TRIAL & ERROR

POEMS BY A ROOKIE

CHEHAK

Made with ♥ on the Notion Press Platform
www.notionpress.com

Contents

Foreword

The first time I ever saw words come to life was when I sneakily read the novels my sister wrote. I gradually moved toward reading published works by various authors and I adored the way I could imagine the words dancing and materializing in front of my eyes.

As I grew up, I fell in love with different aesthetics which pushed me towards poetry. It took a little time but I started appreciating poetry more than any other piece of writing.

The reason why the book states that the contents are "poems by a rookie" is that, well, I am a rookie. And, quite frankly, poetry is difficult to write. To convey feelings in a way that flows, in a way that words feel like waves.

Preface

"We read and write poetry because we are members of the human race. And the human race is filled with passion. And medicine, law, business, engineering, these are noble pursuits and necessary to sustain life. But poetry, beauty, romance, love, these are what we stay alive for."

– Dead Poets Society (1989)

Acknowledgements

My muses, my supporters, and the ones who were always by my side; thank you for helping me make this a reality.

1. 18th

Started out as keyboard class buddies,
Now we are each other's meilleurs amis.
Somewhere between being next door neighbours;
And having thousands of miles between us, we grew up.
We shared beautiful moments,
Memories shine so brightly; we bask in their glow.
We're each other's constants,
And although we may not be next to each other,
I know you've always got my back and I, yours.
And now you're eighteen, an adult at last.
Oh, how time has passed!
Now go get some booze,
Let go of the Sunday blues.
Miss me till we hug again,
Until then, all the worries we shrug.

2. Chaos

Born in a chaotic place,
All I knew was chaos.
They took me someplace peaceful,
Said that I'll find it beautiful.
It is quiet here, maybe more than I'd like,
Traps me in a place where I can't even smile.
I look back and sink into my memories
For all that is left is a melody,
One that reminds me of the chaos I still perceive.

3. City Set to Sink

It's the city of dreams,
With a million lifelines.
The city where the sun doesn't seem to set,
Trains running round the clock.
If you're quiet enough, you can hear the waves crashing on the shore,
If not, you just hear the "shor".
The city is busy and full of life,
No time to wait, no second to spare.
It's a city full of hope and tears,
A city destined to sink.

4. Dear Stranger

Dear stranger, who is no stranger, thank you for waving back at me.
Dear stranger, I'm glad you put Love Me Do by The Beatles in the cafeteria the other day, I thought no-one listened to them anymore.
Dear stranger, I think I've fallen in love with your voice and the way you speak.
Dear stranger, would you please marry me?
Dear stranger, I prefer to call you that since I've never seen this side of you. How could you be so cruel? I'm praying that we could go back to being strangers.
Dear stranger, why do you wound me so? Dear stranger, goodbye.
Dear stranger, it's been years since we met.
Dear stranger, I tried so hard not to cry when I saw you but my eyes betrayed me and made me think about the 'once upon a time' we shared.

5. Grows Deeper

My love for you grows deeper every single day.
And with every time I feel your gaze on me,
There's a surge of warmth in me again.
The number of things that I love about you are endless;
Your laugh – so full of life,
Your embrace – like a cozy blanket on a rainy day,
Your lips and the way you say my name,
Your eyes – the way they look at me, the way they hold so many feelings,
Your hands – oh, the way they hold my heart and my hand at the same time,
Your fingers and the way they trace my soul,
And this was me just getting started with the list that goes till infinity.
My love keeps growing and growing and I don't know how to make you believe,
You're all that's in my heart, mind, body, and soul.
You've captivated me fully and I intend to keep it that way.
I don't wish to be away from you for a moment,
I don't wish to be anything else but yours.

6. Hides & Resides

Love hides and resides in the little things,
It's in knowing their habits,
Knowing what they're feeling without them uttering a word,
It's in knowing their schedule.
It's in knowing someone inside-out and yet finding new things together.
Love does not limit to an "I love you",
It goes much beyond that.
All of these have love hidden in them
– "How are you?", "tell me", "I hope you sleep well" –
They hold much more love than those three magical words do.

7. Hold

Hold my hand tight and never let go.
Hold it with confidence, depicting all love.
Hold my hand while we share things, while we sit in silence.
I could spend all day and all life with you.
Honestly, I love you a little recklessly.
I want to experience new things and redo the old ones.
I want to share every detail with you.
You are my beloved and I hope I'm yours;
And may our story be full of adventures and romance.

8. How?

How is it that you've grown up together,
Always by each other's side,
And still enjoy each other's company?
How is it that you haven't grown tired of them?
How is it that you don't feel inferior?
That you haven't got anything to prove?
How are you two so okay being around each other twenty four seven?
How have the countless comparisons not hurt you?
How is your bond so strong?
How is it that I'm so jealous that I never had that?
That I cannot fathom something like that existing?

9. Imprint / Fade

Poetry lasts for a moment;
It's fleeting, never permanent.
Poetry is beauty and art;
It's a moment of quiet in a world of chaos.
It's someone's story, someone's love,
Someone's appreciation, someone's contempt.
It's just words that used to be feelings;
They may wither, they may fade, they may stay.

10. It's & So

Love is so complicated yet so simple.
It's stealing glances in a room full of people,
And it's also saying "I do" in front of them.
It's the silence they share,
And it's also their loud laughter.
It's sitting in the back seat and holding hands under the table,
It's also walking hand-in-hand for the world to witness.
It's sharing music, stories, heart and soul.
It's trust and time.
It's the ever-lasting spark,
And it is also the effort and desire.
It's so natural yet so confusing.
It's a few soft words,
It's a poem and a letter.
It's a whisper and yet a scream.
It's the delicate touch,
It's the hug that feels like home.
It's so intense, so much more than just a few words.

11. Kids

There once were two kids,
One rational and the other a hopeless romantic.
Used to live in their separate worlds, barely mingled,
Now a part of each other's tiny universe.
The romantic writes this love letter, hoping she'd be less cheesy than usual.
So much for being the 'one who puts her emotions into words'.
She can't even think of them when she's around him,
Wondering how she still gets butterflies when he says her name;
She wants to tell him she feels safe with him,
Feels at home when he's there.
Looks at their shared space as a 'no judgment zone',
Where they both can be who they are.
But will she ever voice these words?
Or will she let them remain in this sorry excuse of a poem?

12. Letter

A letter that feels like a hug,
Words that feel like home.
Feelings as though taking form from paper,
Fleeing into your heart.
The smile on your face as you read it,
The smile on mine as I watch you react.
Your name in the first line,
Mine at the end.
Sentences sing in harmony,
Alphabets a string of melody.
A letter that feels like a hug,
Words that feel like home.

13. Love & Thunder

Thunder is loud & scary, but not scarier than love;
Love is loud & silent, it is expressive & mute.
Thunder is chaperoned by lightning & sparks;
Just like the glimmer and glitter of love.
Thunder is sudden, has no pace;
The way love sees nothing but love itself.

14. Lovers

There was a girl who lived in her own little perfect bubble of music, books and movies.
She had been hurt before many times.
She had built walls around her, not letting anybody in.
She had lost faith in trust.
But then a boy came along.
Her very own blue-eyed boy.
He spent time with her, made her feel like herself again.
Slowly and steadily the walls around her started to break.
For the first time in years, she had let somebody in.
He fell for her. She fell for him.
Everything was going well.
But one day, he suddenly left without saying a word to her.
No reason ever disclosed, no investigation ever done.
In all the funeral chaos,
Nobody noticed the red drops on the maroon carpet.

15. Noise

You wonder why I like noise,
Yet you never ask me.
But I am yet another stubborn soul and I won't let it be.
These noises are the one keeping me sane,
They drown it all though the traces remain.
Don't tell me to let it out, I trust none.
Don't judge me for it, I'll come undone.
Our problems are different,
So is our pain.
Don't belittle mine, I can't do this again.
I stay silent throughout,
Yet all my head does is shout.

16. Reality

(a haiku)

You joke and you laugh;
You're broken, no one sees;
All you are is fake.

17. Unfurl

You're always lifting up other people,
Always being optimistic and joyful for the lot.
You're just giving and giving, expecting nothing in return,
You're always there to lend an ear.
You're warm for others, cold to self,
Towards your feelings, you turn deaf.
Undermining and overthinking,
Keeping your head churning.
Can't you see the reality, my darling?
Can't you see your worth?
Can't you take a break from sparring?
Always finding the worst in yourself,
Always thinking you're no good.
For the heavens, for once,
Look in the mirror and see what others see;
See that kind and beautiful soul,
See her and know that no matter what you may think,
You deserve the joy and spark,
The roses and glitter to leave a mark.
You deserve all the love in the world.
Gently, just let your heart unfurl.

18. You're

Even if I say 'I love you' a thousand times to you,
It'd just be a tiny fraction of what I truly feel.
You've built a home in my heart.
I admire you for who you are,
And you really wouldn't be insecure if you see you through me.
You're my safe haven,
The person I want to lay under the stars with and kiss in the rain.
No amount of words would ever be enough for me to explain what's in my heart,
But that surely doesn't mean that I won't give it a shot.
I wish I could write like Wordsworth and Keats,
And tell you that without you, I cannot breathe.
But today is not the day to be that cheesy;
Nor is it the day to speak through someone else's words.
Thus, I'd like you to know that
You're where I feel safe and loved,
You're someone who makes me feel that everything is okay,
You're the one I can't stay mad at for long,
The one I write poems and letters for.
But lo & behold the truth, you're not mine, nor am I yours.

Author's Notes

Thank you for reading, and I do hope that you enjoyed this tiny little collection of poems.

9 798888 837481

Printed by Libri Plureos GmbH in Hamburg,
Germany